THE WORLD'S TOP TEN

ISLANDS

Neil Morris

ILLUSTRATED BY VANESSA CARD

Belitha Press

Words in **bold** are explained in the glossary
on pages 30–31.

First published in the UK in 1995 by
Belitha Press Limited
31 Newington Green, London N16 9PU

Copyright in this format © Belitha Press 1995
Text copyright © Neil Morris 1995
Illustrations copyright © Vanessa Card 1995

ISBN 1 85561 385 9

British Library Cataloguing in Publication Data for this
book is available from the British Library.

Editor: Claire Edwards
Designer: Dawn Apperley
Picture researcher: Juliet Duff
Consultant Elizabeth M Lewis

Manufactured in China for Imago

Picture acknowledgements: Bryan and Cherry Alexander
9, 10, 17, 18, 24, 25, 26, 27; First Light Associated
Photographers 29 bottom; FLPA 29 top F.Polking;
Nicholas Grimshaw and Partners 23 bottom Peter Cook;
Robert Harding Picture Library 5, 11, 13 bottom, 15, 20,
21, 28 both; NHPA 16 Stephen Krasemann; Still Pictures
4 Andy Crump, 8 B&C Alexander, 13 top Chris Caldicott,
14 T.Thomas, 19 Paul Harrison; TRIP 23 top Peter Rauter.

Contents

What is an island?

An island is a piece of land that is surrounded by water. The biggest islands are all in oceans and seas. But there are many smaller islands in lakes and rivers. Greenland is the biggest island in the world. Australia and Antarctica are also surrounded by water, but they are too big to be called islands. We call them **continents** instead.

Island countries

Some islands, such as Madagascar or the Maldives, form a country. But islands are not always separate countries. Some, such as Greenland, are part of another country. Others, such as New Guinea, are divided between more than one country.

This is one of the 1200 small coral islands in the Indian Ocean that make up the country of the Maldives. Their highest point is only 3 metres, so if the level of the ocean rose slightly, the islands would disappear. People live on 203 of the islands.

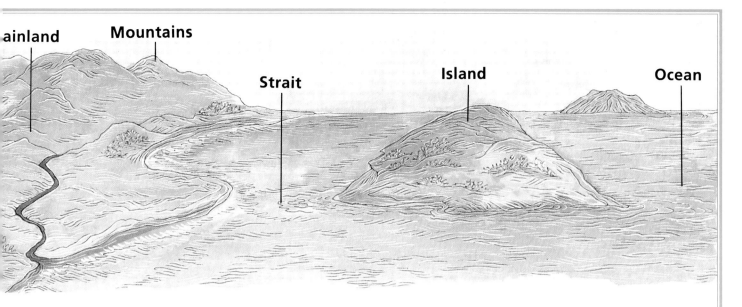

Labels on image: Mainland · Mountains · Strait · Island · Ocean

How islands form

Some islands were formed when movements in the earth's **crust** forced the sea bed to rise and land was pushed up out of the water. So, many islands are really the tops of underwater mountains. Other islands appeared when the sea level rose and flooded low-lying land. The higher areas were left as islands.

Volcanic islands form when underwater volcanoes erupt and make **lava cones** that reach above the sea. In 1963 fishermen saw the island of Surtsey, near Iceland, appear in this way.

The illustrations above and below show the same island, lying in an ocean off a mainland. The cross section below shows how the island is attached to the land beneath the sea.

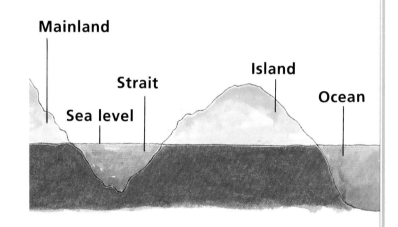

Labels on image: Mainland · Sea level · Strait · Island · Ocean

This erupting Hawaiian volcano looks like a giant firework display. The islands of Hawaii are really the tops of volcanoes.

The biggest islands

In this book we take a look at the ten biggest islands in the world. We see how different they are from each other and get to know the people and animals who have made them their home.

The biggest islands

The map shows where the ten biggest islands are in the world. The biggest of all is Greenland, which is over ten times larger than Victoria, the tenth in the list. These two islands, together with Baffin and Ellesmere, lie in the cold Arctic Ocean. Great Britain is in the Atlantic, and Madagascar and Sumatra are in the warm Indian Ocean. New Guinea, Borneo and Honshu are all in the world's largest ocean, the Pacific.

The world's top ten islands

1	Greenland	2 175 600 sq km
2	New Guinea	821 030 sq km
3	Borneo	744 366 sq km
4	Madagascar	587 041 sq km
5	Baffin Island	476 068 sq km
6	Sumatra	473 607 sq km
7	Honshu	230 448 sq km
8	Great Britain	218 041 sq km
9	Ellesmere Island	212 688 sq km
10	Victoria Island	212 198 sq km

Greenland

Greenland is the largest island in the world. It lies between the North Atlantic and Arctic oceans, off the coast of North America. The island belongs to Denmark, but the people of Greenland, called Greenlanders, govern themselves.

ARCTIC OCEA

Arctic tern

Walrus

Polar bear

Caribou

BAFFIN BAY

Arctic fox

Icebergs

Seals

Narwhal

Mount Gunnbjorn

ARCTIC CIRC

NUUK

Inuit paddling canoe

ATLANTIC Oc

On the north-west coast, the snow-covered **icecap** reaches right to the sea. This stretch of cold sea, called Baffin Bay, separates Greenland from Baffin Island. It is full of small **icebergs**.

Land of the midnight sun

Most of Greenland lies above the **Arctic Circle**, and its northern coast reaches closer to the North Pole than any other land area in the world. The island is almost completely covered by an icecap that is more than 3000 metres thick in places. There are no big roads, and people travel by sea, by air, or across ice-covered land on **snowmobiles** or sledges pulled by dogs.

In the north, the sun hardly sets during the summer months, so there is daylight all the time.

The Inuit people

The first people to settle here were hunters who crossed from North America about 5000 years ago. These people are sometimes called Eskimos, a word that means 'eaters of raw meat'. They prefer to be called **Inuit**, which in their own language means 'people'. Today most Greenlanders are a mixture of Inuit and Scandinavians. The language of Greenland is an Inuit **dialect**.

Why 'green land'?

The island was named by a Viking called Erik the Red, who arrived there in the tenth century. Erik found summer grass growing near the shore of the huge island and named it Greenland. He hoped that this name would attract more **settlers** from Iceland.

Today most of the islanders live near the coast, where there is some ice-free land. On the south coast people graze sheep and cows and grow a few crops, such as potatoes and cabbages. But even here Greenland is not very green.

An Inuit mother carries her son on her back in a special hood. The hood and the woman's clothes are made of warm sealskin.

9

New Guinea

The second largest island in the world lies in the Pacific Ocean, just south of the **Equator** and north of Australia. New Guinea is a very mountainous island and covered in forests.

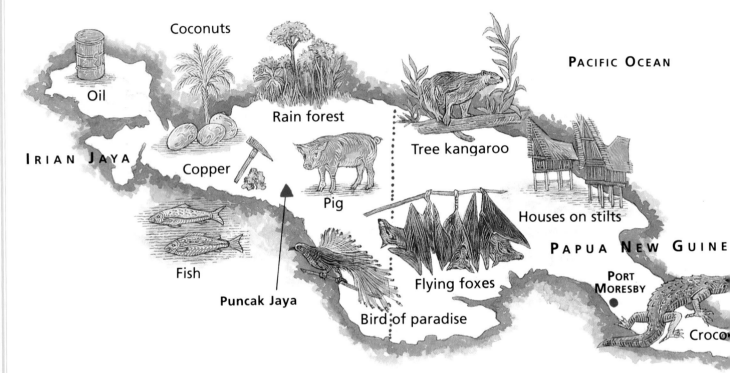

Coconuts

Oil

Rain forest

PACIFIC OCEAN

Tree kangaroo

IRIAN JAYA

Copper

Pig

Houses on stilts

PAPUA NEW GUINE

Fish

Flying foxes

PORT MORESBY

Puncak Jaya

Bird of paradise

Croco

Part of Indonesia

New Guinea and its peoples are divided into two nations. The western half, called Irian Jaya, belongs to Indonesia. In the highlands many people live in small villages of up to five families. The villages are surrounded by gardens, where the people grow **sweet potatoes** and keep pigs

Recently large deposits of oil, **nickel** and copper have been discovered, and soon modern industry may change the islanders' lives.

This village in Irian Jaya is surrounded by **rain for** Women and children live in small round huts, wh are well thatched to keep out the rain. The men in a larger house at the centre of the village.

Papua New Guinea

The island's eastern half, called Papua New Guinea, is a separate country. Here many village houses are built on stilts, so that the people are safe from floods during the rainy season. More and more forest people are moving to the towns along the coast. Today almost 200 000 people live in the nation's capital city, Port Moresby.

Houses stand on stilts on the waterfront at Port Moresby. The capital of Papua New Guinea is also the country's main port.

Rain forest and peoples

New Guinea's rain forests contain valuable wood such as teak and mahogany. But in some areas these trees are being cut down faster than they can be planted.

The island is home to many peoples who speak hundreds of different languages. The first to settle there were Negritos, people who are similar to African **Pygmies** and are usually less than 1.5 metres tall.

Borneo

Borneo, the world's third largest island, belongs to three countries. Kalimantan, to the south and east, is part of Indonesia. In the north, Sarawak and Sabah are both states of Malaysia. On the north coast there is a tiny country called Brunei.

Mount Kinabalu

Rhi

SABAH

BRUNEI

Natural gas

Proboscis monkey

Oil

Asian elephant

SARAWAK

Rain forest

Sarawak Cavern

Hornbill

Orang-utan

KALIMANTAN

Dayak longhouse

EQUATOR

Rubber trees

Leopard

Bananas

BANJERMASIN

Man of the forest

The island has many mountain ranges and is covered by rain forest. Borneo lies on the Equator, so it is always warm. There is rain all year round, and it is very wet during the **monsoon** season, from October to March.

The **tropical** climate is ideal for the orang-utan. This ape is one of our closest animal relatives, and in the Malay language its name means 'man of the forest'. But the rain forest where the orang-utan lives is being cut down for **timber**. Special **reserves** have been set up to protect it.

FACTS

AREA	744 366 sq km
LOCATION	Pacific Ocean
POPULATION	12 000 000
BIGGEST CITY	Banjermasin
HIGHEST POINT	Mount Kinabalu, 4101m

Longhouses and caves

Many tribes of the Dayak people still live in a traditional way. As many as 50 families may live together in a wooden longhouse. These houses, which are sometimes more than 200 metres long, are built on stilts to protect them from monsoon floods.

In the north of the island there is a great network of caves. The Sarawak Cavern is the biggest **cave chamber** in the world. It is 700 metres long – as long as seven football pitches.

Some parts of the Borneo rain forest have hardly changed over millions of years. The trees grow close together, and some are more than 30 metres high.

Sultan of Brunei

Brunei is a sultanate, which means a country ruled by a sultan. This small nation owns large reserves of oil and natural gas. Over three-quarters of Brunei's money comes from the sale of oil. The island buys most of its food from other countries.

The Sultan of Brunei is said to be the richest person in the world. He lives in a fantastic palace (above) on the island.

Madagascar

The fourth largest island in the world lies in the Indian Ocean, off the coast of Africa. Madagascar is a land of contrasts and surprises. There is tropical rain forest on the east coast, but in the south it is hot and dry. The climate is cooler in the mountains that run down the middle of the island.

MOZAMBIQUE CHANNEL

Unique animals

There are many animals and plants that live only on Madagascar. These include tenrecs, which look like hedgehogs, and monkey-like lemurs. Two-thirds of the world's chameleons also live here. These lizards change colour if they are angry or frightened, and some are so tiny they could perch on your thumb.

INDIA
OCEA

Rice

Mount
Maromokotro

Baobab
tree

Chameleon

ANTANANARIVO

Lemur

Tenrec

Vanilla
pods

Rain forest

Ring-tailed lemurs live only in the scrubland and forests of southern Madagascar. They feed on fruit, leaves, bark and grass, and live in troops of up to 40 animals.

Malagasy people

The people of Madagascar are called Malagasy. Some of the earliest of the island's inhabitants arrived more than 1500 years ago from South-East Asia. Others crossed the Mozambique Channel from the African mainland.

The Asian settlers, called the Merina, once ruled the island. Today most of them live near Antananarivo, the island's capital city, while the Africans live mainly along the coast.

All the island's people speak the same language, which is also called Malagasy. Madagascar belonged to France for over 50 years and many people still speak French, especially in the cities. The island became independent in 1960.

Farmers use cattle to plough the fields, before planting the wet ground with rice. The island has plenty of rain in the monsoon season.

Farming the land

Most of the people make their living as farmers. Many grow just enough food for themselves and their families. The main crops are rice, **cassava**, sugar cane, coffee and vanilla. Farmers also raise cattle and catch fish. Rice is the Malagasies' main food, while coffee and vanilla are sold to other countries. These are called **cash crops**.

FACTS

AREA	587 041 sq km
LOCATION	Indian Ocean
POPULATION	11 197 000
BIGGEST CITY	Antananarivo
HIGHEST POINT	Mount Maromokotro 2885m

Baffin Island

Canada has many islands off the northern coast of its mainland, in the Arctic Ocean. Baffin is the largest of these Canadian islands. Three-quarters of the island's people are Inuit.

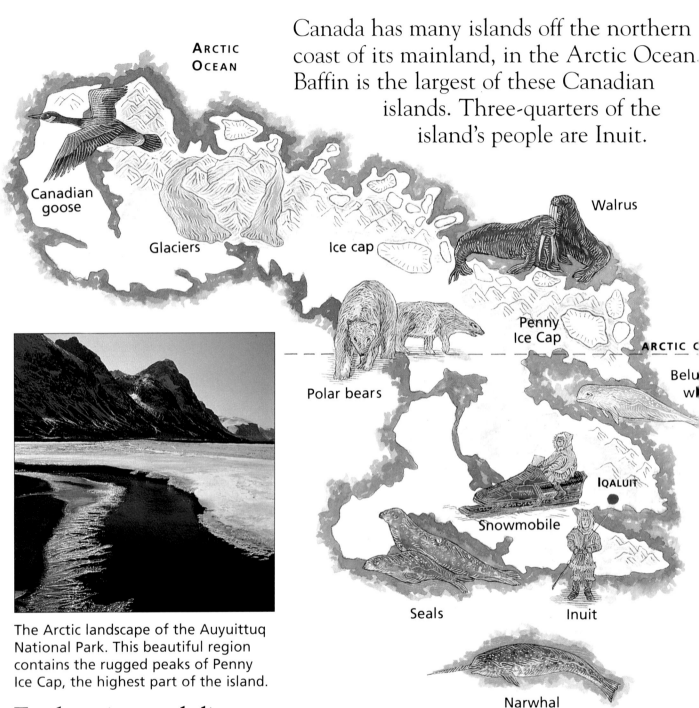

ARCTIC
OCEAN

Canadian goose

Glaciers

Ice cap

Walrus

Penny
Ice Cap

ARCTIC O

Polar bears

Belu
w

IQALUIT

Snowmobile

Seals

Inuit

Narwhal

The Arctic landscape of the Auyuittuq National Park. This beautiful region contains the rugged peaks of Penny Ice Cap, the highest part of the island.

Exploration and discovery

The Inuit people made the Arctic region their home thousands of years ago. About 1000 years ago, a Viking called Leif Eriksson discovered an island and called it Helluland. The name means 'land of the flat stones'.

This was probably Baffin Island, which was later named after the English sailor William Baffin. European explorers found glittering rocks here, and thought they had discovered gold. It turned out to be worthless **fool's gold**.

Inuit homeland

Baffin is part of the North-West Territories of Canada. In 1992 the people of this region voted for a large part of it to become an Inuit homeland. In 1999 Baffin will become part of the territory of Nunavut, which means 'our land' in the Inuit language.

   The largest settlement on Baffin is Iqaluit, which has only 3000 inhabitants. At the end of April each year, there is a festival in Iqaluit, with beard-growing competitions, igloo-building, snowmobile races and traditional Inuit singing and dancing.

Children play outside their school in Iqaluit. The playground is covered in snow and ice for most of the year.

FACTS

AREA	476 068 sq km
LOCATION	Arctic Ocean
POPULATION	10 000
BIGGEST SETTLEMENT	Iqaluit
HIGHEST POINT	Penny Ice Cap 2591m

Lakes and ice caps

Baffin Island is cold and mountainous. It has **glaciers**, icecaps and **fjords**. White whales, called belugas, swim in the icy waters around Baffin, especially in Cumberland **Sound**.

   On the east coast there are cliffs more than 2000 metres high. Much of the island is only free of ice in the summer months of June, July and August.

Sumatra

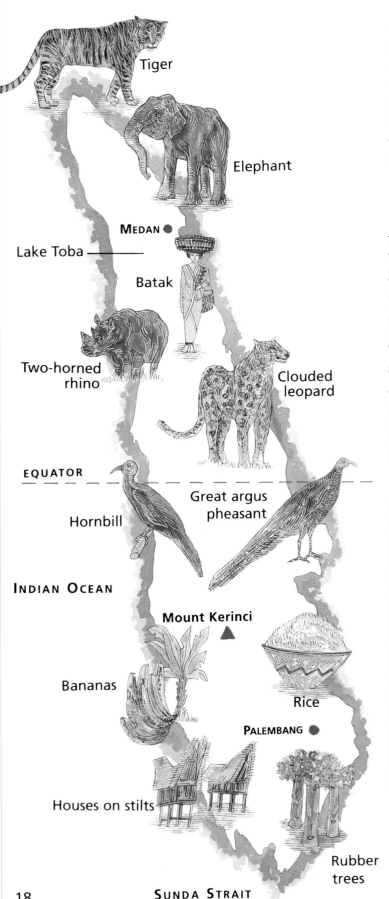

Tiger

Elephant

MEDAN ●

Lake Toba

Batak

Two-horned rhino

Clouded leopard

EQUATOR

Great argus pheasant

Hornbill

INDIAN OCEAN

Mount Kerinci ▲

Bananas

Rice

PALEMBANG ●

Houses on stilts

Rubber trees

SUNDA STRAIT

Sumatra is an Indonesian island that, like Borneo, lies on the Equator. Sumatra is separated from another Indonesian island, Java, by a narrow stretch of sea called the Sunda **Strait**.

Moving between islands

Sumatra is more than three times larger than Java, but far fewer people live there. The Indonesian government has offered free land for small farms in the southern region of Sumatra, to encourage Javanese to move to the island. Most Sumatrans live outside towns, but more than 2 million people live in the largest city, called Medan.

Most Menangkabau people live in villages. This one is in Sumatra's tropical highlands. Some villages have only a few houses, while others may have several hundred.

Followers of Islam

Many Sumatran people still live traditional lives. The Menangkabau people live in valleys between high mountains, where they grow rice in terraced fields. The tropical climate helps them grow chilli peppers, cloves, cassava and bananas. They are also skilful wood-carvers and weavers.

Like most Indonesians, the Menangkabau are Muslims, followers of the religion of Islam. Many of the island's Batak people are now Christians. Their traditional home is Lake Toba, in the north of the island.

This busy market is in Palembang, Sumatra's second largest city, in the south of the island. Farmers bring their vegetables to markets like this to sell them to city people.

FACTS

AREA	473 607 sq km
LOCATION	Indian Ocean
POPULATION	36 882 000
BIGGEST CITY	Medan
HIGHEST POINT	Mount Kerinci, 3806m

Sumatran animals

There are many rare animals in Sumatra. But as humans move into areas where the animals live, they destroy their natural **habitat**. The Sumatran tiger, the Sumatran rhinoceros (also called the Asian two-horned or hairy rhino), the Sumatran elephant and the beautiful clouded leopard are now all **endangered species**.

There may be only 400 Sumatran tigers left on the island. Although tigers are now protected by law, people still hunt them.

Honshu

Japan is made up of four main islands and nearly 4000 smaller ones. Honshu is the largest island and makes up well over half of Japan's land area. More than three-quarters of Japanese people live there.

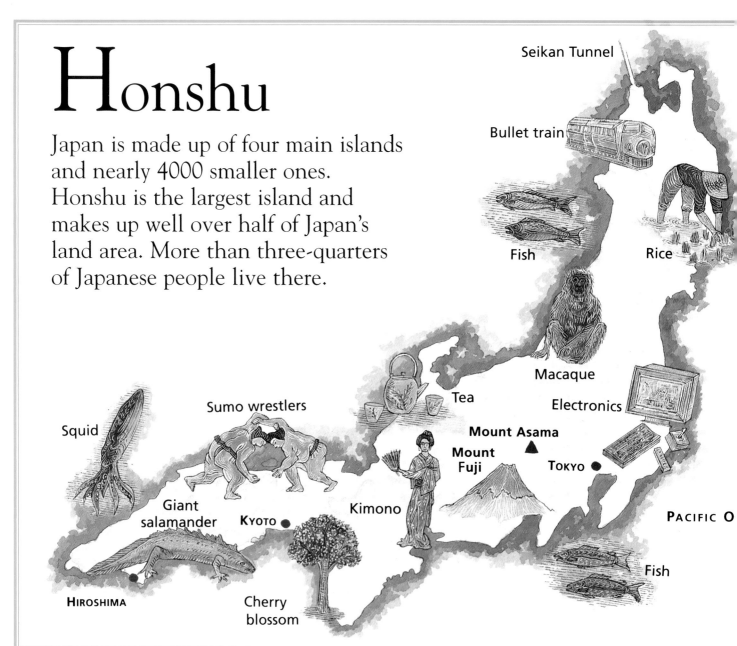

Seikan Tunnel

Bullet train

Fish

Rice

Macaque

Squid

Sumo wrestlers

Tea

Electronics

Mount Asama

Mount Fuji

TOKYO ●

Giant salamander

KYOTO ●

Kimono

PACIFIC O

HIROSHIMA

Cherry blossom

Fish

Volcanoes and earthquakes

Millions of years ago volcanoes on the floor of the Pacific Ocean **erupted** and formed underwater mountains. These grew higher and eventually formed the islands of Japan. Today there are still many volcanoes and earthquakes in this region. In 1923 and 1995 terrible earthquakes killed or injured thousands of people on Honshu. Mount Asama, in the middle of the island, is an active volcano that could erupt at any time.

These rice fields are on different levels, so water can flow down from one to the other. Farmers plant the rice during the rainy season.

Old and new

Tokyo is the capital city of Japan and the largest city on Honshu. It is the second biggest city in the world, after Mexico City, with over 18 million inhabitants. There are another seven cities on Honshu that have more than a million people living in each. These include Hiroshima, the city that was destroyed by the world's first **atomic bomb** in 1945.

Honshu is a centre for business and industry. The cities are crowded and modern, but tradition is also important. Many ancient forms of drama are still popular in Japan. **Bunraku** is a puppet play, in which each large puppet is operated by three puppeteers (see below). In **noh** drama the actors wear wooden masks, and in **kabuki** the characters have cleverly painted faces.

FACTS

AREA	230 448 sq km
LOCATION	Pacific Ocean
POPULATION	100 000 000
BIGGEST CITY	Tokyo
HIGHEST POINT	Mount Fuji, 3776m

The Akihabara district of Tokyo is full of shops selling electronic goods. Japan is a world leader in the production of computers, hi-fi equipment and television sets.

Connecting islands

Since 1988 the people of Honshu have been able to travel to Japan's next largest island, Hokkaido, through the world's longest tunnel. The Seikan rail tunnel is almost 54 kilometres long.

21

Great Britain

Great Britain is the largest of the British islands. It is made up of England, Scotland and Wales, and is part of the United Kingdom of Great Britain and Northern Ireland.

Highlands and lowlands

The name Great Britain has been used since 1603, when King James of Scotland also became King of England and Wales. The word 'great' was used to mean 'big'.

Much of Scotland is covered by the Grampians and the North-West Highlands, which are wild, mountainous areas. Wales and the north of England are hilly, with low **fertile** land in the valleys and near the coast. The south and east of England are much flatter. There are more towns, cities and motorways in the lowland parts of England than anywhere else in Great Britain.

Fishing

Deer

Cod

SCOTLAND

Salmon

NORTH SEA

Ben Nevis

Oil

Scottish piper

Plaice

Football

ATLANTIC OCEAN

Cricket

Welsh costume

ENGLAND

WALES

Sheep

Big Ben

Puffin

LONDON

Dairy cattle

Stonehenge

Channel Tu...

Mackerel

Sailing

FACTS

AREA	218 041 sq km
LOCATION	Atlantic Ocean
POPULATION	55 800 000
BIGGEST CITY	London
HIGHEST POINT	Ben Nevis, 1343m

Scotland has many beautiful lakes called **lochs**. The lochs are all long and deep. Loch Shiel (above) is 28 kilometres long, 128 metres deep, and only 1.4 kilometres wide.

Rich history

Over 500 years ago ships left this island to carry explorers and traders all over the globe. A hundred years ago a huge empire was ruled from Britain, and a fifth of the world's people were governed by English laws and **customs**.

In about 1750 the Industrial Revolution began in Britain. The old ways of life based on small farms and home crafts began to change as factories and industrial cities grew up all over the island. Today, farming is still important, but farms are bigger and worked by modern machinery.

Continental link

Today Great Britain has close links with the continent of Europe. The United Kingdom is part of the European Union, which brings governments and business people closer together. In 1994 the Channel Tunnel opened. This rail tunnel is almost 50 kilometres long and connects England with France. It is the second longest tunnel in the world after the Seikan tunnel in Japan.

'Le Shuttle' trains waiting in London to travel to the coast and through the Channel Tunnel to France. They have a top speed of 160 kph.

Ellesmere Island

Ellesmere is the furthest north of the Canadian islands, and lies well above the Arctic Circle. It is separated from Greenland by a narrow sea channel.

Cold desert

Ellesmere has an unusual climate. It has less rain than parts of the Sahara Desert. It is cold all year round, and the winters are long and dark. From November till March there is no sunlight at all. Despite its iciness, the island is not covered in deep snow.

The landscape here is called **tundra**. Only the top few centimetres of frozen earth thaw in the summer. There are no trees, but in summer Arctic flowers, **sedges** and heather grow on the island.

Lemmings

Arctic fox

Lake Hazen

Barbeau Peak

Musk ox

Snow

EUREKA

Heather

Arctic wolf

Polar b

ARCTI OCEA

Arctic hare

GRISE FJORD

Cotton grass grows near Lake Hazen, in late summer. The plant's name comes from its silky hairs that look like cotton. In summer the surface of the tundra becomes very boggy. Canadians call this swampy ground muskeg.

Settlements

The only place where islanders live all the time is in the far south, at Grise Fjord. About 100 Inuit live there. They call their settlement Ausuittuq or 'the place where it never thaws'.

Further north is the Eureka radio station, run by Canada and the USA. **Fossilized** forests have been found in this area. They tell us that millions of years ago the region's climate must have been much warmer. At the most northerly tip of the island is the Alert weather station.

FACTS

AREA	212 688 sq km
LOCATION	Arctic Ocean
POPULATION	100
BIGGEST SETTLEMENT	Grise Fjord (Ausuittuq)
HIGHEST POINT	Barbeau Peak, 2600m

National park

A large part of the north of the island is now a Canadian national park. Here there are mountains, glaciers and even a lake. Musk oxen, caribou, Arctic foxes, wolves, **lemmings** and more than 30 species of birds live here, undisturbed by humans. There are many Arctic hares too. The colour of their coat changes to match their surroundings. In winter, the hare's coat is as white as snow.

Park wardens help to release a Peary caribou back to the wild. They have fitted it with a special collar so that they can follow its movements by **satellite**.

Victoria Island

Victoria is the third largest of the Canadian Arctic islands and the tenth largest island in the world. It was named after Queen Victoria of England, 150 years ago. Cambridge Bay and Holman are the only two settlements on the island.

Musk ox

ARCTIC OCE

Polar bear

Inuit wi
dog tea

Inuit carving

Eider duck

HOLMAN

Walrus

Arctic flowers

CAMBRIDGE BA

Caribou

Arctic char

A sailing boat lies on the frozen beach at Holman, on the west coast. This settlement began as an Inuit community. Now there is a hotel that takes 16 tourists.

Good place to fish

The main settlement on Victoria Island is at Cambridge Bay, which was named by English traders in 1839. Inuit people once used this area as a summer camp. They call it Ikaluktutiak, which means 'a good place to fish'.

Today there is a canning factory to **process** Arctic char, a type of fish caught in the freezing cold ocean, and a modern wind-powered **generating plant**. Cambridge Bay also has an old stone church, and a visitors' centre for the new Arctic Coast Tourist Association. Inuit arts and crafts are sold at the Ikaluktutiak store.

The North-West Passage

For centuries, European explorers tried to find a way from the Atlantic to the Pacific Ocean by sailing round the north coast of North America. In 1846 an Englishman named John Franklin sailed almost as far as Victoria Island. Then his two ships became trapped in ice and he and his 129 men died.

In 1906 Roald Amundsen, a Norwegian, followed the same route and sailed past Victoria's south coast in his ship *Gjöa*. He sailed on to discover the North-West Passage to the Pacific through the Bering Strait. His ship from a later voyage still lies half-sunk in Cambridge Bay harbour.

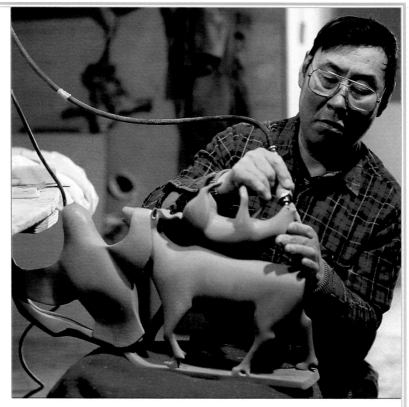

Holman is famous for its Inuit art centre. **Soapstone** is traditionally carved with chisels and files and then polished. Today more modern tools are often used.

FACTS

AREA	212 198 sq km
LOCATION	Arctic Ocean
POPULATION	1300
BIGGEST SETTLEMENT	Cambridge Bay (Ikaluktutiak)
HIGHEST POINT	655m

Cold, flat land

Unlike the other Arctic islands, Victoria has no big mountains, and its highest point is only 655 metres. The island holds the Canadian record for the lowest temperature in midsummer, -3°C. The average midwinter temperature is -31°C. When it is very cold, the island's wild musk oxen huddle together, sheltering their calves in the middle of the herd.

The world's islands

Four of the world's ten largest islands lie off the coast of North America. These Arctic islands are cold, and fewer than 70 000 people live on them. Borneo and Sumatra lie on the Equator and have a hot climate. New Guinea and Madagascar are tropical and warm. Great Britain and Honshu, which are neither very warm nor very cold, have by far the biggest populations. There are many other fascinating and very different islands around the world.

Manhattan

This island lies at the north end of New York Bay, USA. It is one of the five boroughs of New York City and is surrounded by three rivers. Many bridges and tunnels connect the island to the rest of the city. The tallest skyscraper in the photograph is the World Trade Center. Other famous buildings on the island are the Empire State Building and the headquarters of the United Nations. This very crowded island still has room for a big park in the middle, called Central Park.

Islands of Fiji

A close group of islands is called an **archipelago**. There are many archipelagos scattered across the world's biggest ocean, the Pacific. They are grouped together in three regions – Melanesia, Micronesia and Polynesia. The 844 islands of Fiji are in Melanesia. Only 106 of them are inhabited. The larger islands are volcanic, while many tiny **islets** are made of coral.

Galapagos Islands

This group of 15 islands lies on the Equator, in the Pacific Ocean. Although the islands are warm, the ocean here has cold currents. The volcanic islands belong to the nearest mainland country, Ecuador.

People live on only four of the islands, but on all of them there are animals that live nowhere else. These include large groups of marine iguanas, the only lizards that swim in the sea. They feed on seaweed, and then warm up on the islands' volcanic rocks. The iguanas blow sea salt out through their noses in a spray of water vapour.

Manitoulin Island

Not all islands are in the ocean. The largest freshwater island in the world is in Lake Huron, one of the Great Lakes of North America. The lake lies on the border between Michigan, USA, and Ontario, Canada. Manitoulin Island is 129 kilometres long and up to 48 kilometres wide, and is in the Canadian half of the lake.

The island is covered in forest and surrounded by several smaller islands in the lake. Timber and tourism are important to the islanders living here.

Glossary

People hunt tigers for their beautiful coats.

archipelago A group of islands.

Arctic Circle An imaginary circle around the earth near the North Pole.

atomic bomb A nuclear bomb that causes great destruction.

bunraku A Japanese puppet play.

cash crop Plants grown by farmers to sell to others rather than to eat themselves.

cassava A tropical plant. The root is cooked and eaten as a vegetable.

cave chamber A room in a system of underground tunnels.

continent A huge land mass.

crust The earth's outer shell.

custom The usual way of doing things that is handed down over the years.

dialect The form of a language spoken in a particular area.

endangered species Animals or plants that are in danger of dying out.

Equator An imaginary circle around the middle of the earth.

erupt To throw out molten rock, ash and steam with an explosion.

fertile Having rich soil and producing good crops.

fjord A long narrow inlet of the sea.

fool's gold A worthless yellow metal sometimes mistaken for gold.

fossilize Preserve the remains of once-living things from prehistoric times.

generating plant A place where electricity is made.

glacier A mass of permanent ice that moves very slowly.

habitat The natural home of an animal or a plant.

iceberg A mass of ice that floats in the sea.

icecap A thick mass of ice that covers an area of land and never melts.

Bunraku, a traditional Japanese puppet play.

Inuit People of the Arctic region of North America and Greenland, sometimes called Eskimos.

islet A small island.

kabuki A form of Japanese drama based on popular legends.

lava cone A cone-shaped mountain that builds up as molten rock from a volcano hardens.

lemming A small Arctic animal with gnawing teeth.

loch A Scottish lake.

monsoon A wind that brings heavy rains in southern Asia.

nickel A silvery-white metal.

noh A form of Japanese drama with music, dancing and chanting.

process To treat food so that it stays good to eat for a long time.

Pygmies A hunting people of the African rain forest who are very short.

rain forest Thick forest found in warm tropical areas of heavy rainfall.

Musk oxen huddling together on the tundra.

ranch A large cattle farm.

reserve An area set aside to protect the plants and animals that live there.

satellite A device that circles the earth in space and sends back information.

sedge A grass-like plant.

settler A person who goes to live in a new country.

snowmobile A small car with skis instead of wheels.

soapstone A type of soft grey-white stone.

sound A large bay.

strait A narrow sea channel between two areas of land.

sweet potato A tropical plant grown for its root, which people eat.

timber Wood used for building and other purposes.

tropical Found in the tropics, the hottest part of the earth near the Equator.

tundra Treeless plains where the top layer of ground is always frozen.

An orang-utan in the Borneo rain forest.

31

Index

Words in **bold** appear in the glossary on pages 30-31.